MW01077704

Also by Brooks Haxton

Mister
Toebones

Mister Toebones

POEMS

Brooks Haxton

Alfred A. Knopf   New York   2021

THIS IS A BORZOI BOOK PUBLISHED BY ALFRED A. KNOPF

Copyright © 2021 by Brooks Haxton

All rights reserved. Published in the United States by Alfred A. Knopf,
a division of Penguin Random House LLC, New York, and distributed
in Canada by Penguin Random House Canada Limited, Toronto.

www.aaknopf.com

Knopf, Borzoi Books, and the colophon are registered trademarks
of Penguin Random House LLC.

Library of Congress Cataloging-in-Publication Data
Names: Haxton, Brooks, [date] author.
Title: Mister Toebones : poems / Brooks Haxton.
Description: First edition. | New York : Alfred A. Knopf, 2021.
Identifiers: LCCN 2020017755 (print) | LCCN 2020017756 (ebook) |
    ISBN 9780593318522 (hardcover) | ISBN 9780593318539 (ebook)
Subjects: LCGFT: Poetry.
Classification: LCC PS3558.A825 M57 2021 (print) |
    LCC PS3558.A825 (ebook) | DDC 811/.54—dc23
LC record available at https://lccn.loc.gov/2020017755
LC ebook record available at https://lccn.loc.gov/2020017756

Jacket photograph of Richard Haxton by Brooks Haxton
Jacket design by Kelly Blair

Manufactured in Canada
First Edition

To Daniel Moriarty

native brook trout . . . their backs
Purple-black and traced with gray . . . like
Maps, dream maps, like no maps
I could ever hope to draw or follow.

—DANIEL MORIARTY

No, I can't say as ever I was lost, but I was bewildered once
for three days.

—DANIEL BOONE

Contents

Mister
Toebones

Canoe

A damselfly lit on the inside seam at my knee,
her tail tip blue as a blue flame.
She flitted away.

Nothing was settled by now. Nothing was certain.
Ten thousand riffle bugs twitched on the pond.
My boat kept drifting into the cattails.

Another damselfly there lit on the inside seam
at my knee. She flitted. She lit again, on my knuckle.

Everything so far had already happened.
Everything else was about to happen.

Bluegill swam under the boat.
A redfin pickerel hovered and darted away.

Again I had fallen in love
with my wife, when I thought
I might lose her, and I was the one lost.

There was a slow leak in the hull by my foot.
The wind blew hard, and a dragonfly
soared straight into it.

When I tried to row home, the prow
kept swinging about in the wind.

It was easier backwards.
The prow with each stroke dipped
and rocked up wobbling out of the water.

The Other World

They found the skeleton of a man
under the grass at Crooked Lake.
His people left him in his grave
a chariot with spoked wheels
and heads of horses in full tack,
with severed leg bones posed to strut
at the instruction of the dead.

From a burial site of the Eastern
Han comes a galloping horse
in bronze, lips and nostrils
flared, right hind hoof set
on the sturdy back of a swallow
who turns her head as if
surprised to carry him in flight.

Mister Toebones, Called in Several Languages the Reaper

Phalangium opilio

A daddy longlegs on an oak leaf at the cemetery
froze and started bobbing. Children in the country
used to pick these up by one leg. They said,
*Grandfather graybeard, tell me where my cattle are,
or I will kill you.* Where he pointed, waving
with another leg, they looked, and now their names
were chiseled on the stones around me, Grace
and Samuel and Sarah. Mister Toebones
is a name they would have liked: I took it
from the Latin. He quit bobbing. With his second
legs now, which were the longest, he was reaching
into the air for molecules as vivid to his toes
as memories to an old man's brain. I can remember
from my childhood Grace gone quiet
on her deathbed. People say that the daddy longlegs
bears the deadliest known venom. Mister Toebones
bears no venom and bites nobody but little worms
and larvae. My father showed me in the turret
on the reaper's head the two eyes mounted
left and right. With one of these he must
have seen me at my father's grave. He must
have tasted with a bristle on his second
forefoot just a touch of something human.

To Abu Ali al-Hasan ibn al-Hasan ibn al-Haytham

I just found out, Hasan, your full name means
Father of the Most High,
the Good or Handsome,
son again of the Handsome,
son of the Young Eagle.

I am son of Kenneth,
son again of Kenneth,
which means Handsome, like Hasan.

My first name Ellis also, like Ali,
claims God as my salvation.

As for Haxton: in your time, I think,
in Hawks-town, my namesakes trained falcons,
not the Sons of Eagles maybe, but their kin.

Our names are synonyms.
But more than that, Hasan,
though dead a thousand years,
you came to me when I was young.

When I taught children in sixth grade
to make a pinhole camera
from a cardboard box,
with photographic paper for their film,

although I did not know it then,

this was a gift I passed along from you
to them, and inside this
they formed from light their images.

One girl I taught that spring
spiked such a fever in her brain
she died. At twelve from a mosquito bite
she died. They dug her grave nearby
in Minnesota where we lived,
in the state of water mirroring the sky.

But first, Hasan, because of you,
a thousand threads of light
inside the darkness of a little box
preserved this image of her face.

After the Snow Squall

When the crescent
hung in the clear
with Mars and Venus
over the frozen lake,
the dean
in the parking lot
could see
that the darker region
shone from a shimmer
of noon waves
on the Pacific,
so that the lunar lakes
and seas appeared
as brightly Earth-lit
as she had ever seen them,
and she wondered
how she would look
from there,
from the Marsh of Decay
at lunar midnight,
here on the just-past-full
Earth where the edge
had been shaven
into the darkness.

Olm

Proteus anguinus

Salamanders used to live in fire,
but these live underwater, underground,
in bone-cold darkness without air, some of them
for more than a hundred years. They look like snakes
with feet and human skin, the pale snake's head
without a face, inane, all baby pink
and slippery: no eyes that you can see,
no ears, no nose, no mouth, or almost none . . .
gills at the neck, branching on either side,
blood red, like lungs turned inside out. The first
Slovenians who saw these wriggling, flushed
into the light by heavy rains, considered them
human fish. Such human fish, they reasoned,
with such winglike gills, they must have been
the spawn of dragons. Near the olm the earliest
vampire lived, a peasant by the name of Jure
Grando, Big George. He rose from the grave
at night to find his widow, whom he raped
while smiling, she said, from the effort
to draw breath. The neighbors wanted to drive
a stake into his heart, and they tried hawthorn,
which is a hard wood from an enchanted tree
blossoming at the mouth of the cave
into the other world, but hawthorn would not
pierce Big George's heart. The village priest
reminded the corpse, where it lay smiling still
after they dug it up, that Jesus did not suffer

on the cross to make that ghoulish smile
complacent, and a man named Stipan (Steve)
stepped forward, saw in hand. He sawed off
George's head while everybody watched the coffin
fill with blood. The first book to describe this
was the first to describe the olm as well,
The Glory of the Duchy of Carniola, Nuremberg,
1689. When prey is scarce, the olm chillaxes
sometimes, motionless for ten years, to wait.
His heftier cousin in the subterranean lakes
of Central Mexico is called the water monster,
or axolotl . . . monster, here, in the older sense
of cosmic omen, a creature which the indigenous
people find, though near extinction, tasty.

Early in the Christian Empire

Constantine had his first son, commander
of fleets and legions, heir presumptive,
put to death by hanging. Also the empress,
not much older than her stepson, he had
choked by steam in an overheated bath.
This Constantine deemed merciful.
His sons by her he placed years later,
all three, on imperial thrones. Soon
they murdered their most eminent kin.
In a few years the eldest brother fell
in a war to kill the youngest. Then, the death
of the youngest, dragged from hiding
in a church by men supposedly his own
and butchered, left only the one most feared.
Half his army died in the deadliest battle
ever fought by Rome, while he hid nearby:
Church historians have him rapt in prayer.
On his deathbed in a fever, having murdered
the next-to-last of his cousins, he saw,
finally, he was to be succeeded by the last.

The Featherbed

in the presidential suite
was the wettest we've ever seen
from the standpoint of pee.

Copernicus

After he took his priestly vow, my uncle proposed,
they say, to the rector's daughter. She bore his son,
in any case, and married another man. Later
my uncle had me take my vow. Men of the cloth
elected him Prince-Bishop. His son was mayor.
I was a canon for life, and his physician. In my study
at the episcopal palace I translated from Greek
a book of poems in praise of moral truth,
and of the prostitutes and beauties of Byzantium.
I dedicated these to him. At forty I moved
from the palace into the tower of a cathedral
in a fishing village. There, observing the heavens
when I could, I managed coin and property for the state.
My housekeeper when I was old was banished
by my onetime friend, the new Prince-Bishop,
who alleged that she was more to me than I would say.
Devotion, meanwhile, to the loving mind of God
made unacceptable the nest of calibrated rings
with Earth at the center and a tiny Sun in orbit.
This, the science of a thousand years, I took
in hand, to measure by its rule my thought,
to set aside the old, ungainly universe, and leave
God's body true to its own motion naked.

We Could Say Οὐρανός

Whoever thinks that *urinous*
has canceled the pun in *your anus*
needs a clue: with *oo* from *clue*
and *awss* from *sauce* we could
say *oor-a-NAWSS*. Homer
said that, and he did not need to see
to call a god by name. Those
who could see Ouranos back then
saw only a speck. Nobody knew
the speck was a planet. Nobody
knew what planets were.
Ouranos was a blue-green orb
spun backwards on its side
with an aurora at its belt and moons
and rings and a magnetic field
warped every which way. Winds blow
stronger there than storms that upend
double-wides in Kansas. Once in a while
a meteor big as I am, older maybe
than the Moon, sails into a wind
like that, and burns, and flashes,
oblivious, under a cloud of ice.

Sea Cave

Beyond the mouth of a stairwell
they may find under the sweep
of their dive lights blue crab
and American lobster, swimming
sideways, swimming backwards,
walking the platform where I walked
among the millions brought and left
and carried away aboard the IRT.

Catullus, Carmen III

Mourn, O gods of love and mortal lovers.
Mourn. My girlfriend's sparrow, apple
of her eye, is dead, the one she dandled
in her lap, and let hop here and there
with little chirps of joy, sweet thing—now
gone that dark way none comes home.
For this I curse you, dark one, swallower
of beauty: for the dark deed which has made
my girl's eyes red with weeping.

Catullus, Carmen VIII

Enough, Catullus! No more pleading!
What you thought went wrong went
wrong. When days were sunnier,
and when a girl was willing, you made love.
You loved her, let's just say, as none
may evermore be loved. You gave her
all you had. She laughed, and what she gave
you took, and it was brilliant. Now,
when she wants nothing more, your
pleading least of all, stand firm. Say:
Goodbye, girl. Catullus is unmoved.
He does not care now what you do.
If no one cares, it serves you right,
you bitch! Now see who finds your teasing
sweet, who begs for it, who praises it,
who kisses you, who whispers you
your name . . . And whose lips are you biting?
Not mine. No: Catullus is unmoved.

Essential Tremor

FOR DANIEL MORIARTY

The black and gold stitch
from the upper gill of a brook trout
to the middle ray of the tail fin,
you once told me, houses hair cells
sensitive to the flow of the stream.
And the rest . . . that dark green
swath on the flank,
the spots of ocher, stipples
blood red ringed with cornflower blue . . .
the whole thing shimmering
with the most delicate scales,
to the fisherman's eye
is a revelation. You too,
after you led me down at dusk
into a stream so cold
it made my ankles hurt,
and after we caught one each,
just big enough to keep
and cook on a little fire we made
at the foot of the mountain
under the Dog Day stars, you too,
when you smiled, freckles by firelight
trembling on the back of your hand.

To Josephine Chamberlain Ayres Haxton

From the end of the gravel road
we walked down into the woods
to look for a swimming hole in the creek.

You kept scanning the ground for trilliums
you said you wanted to plant
on the way to the house
where your father spent his childhood.

In the gulley we saw handprints
of opossums, and the pad marks from raccoon
and fox and rabbit, scribbled over
with mouse and bird tracks.

There were chanterelles at the foot of a beech trunk,
and in the cleft of a root a copperhead
rearing to strike, bands on her back
almost as orange as the mushrooms.

She came sidewinding straight at you, rattling
her tail in the fallen beech leaves, belly
big with eggs about to hatch inside her.

If I had written you this when you could read,
you might have reminded me that your friend
Bert came on our walk to the creek. I loved Bert.

She was delighted, as usual, by the woods and you.
It was a good day, though we found no swimming hole
or trilliums. None of us got bitten by the snake.

The creek lay sunlit in the deep woods,
brilliant, rippling over the sand and gravel,
with clear pools here and there to the knee,
where crawdads swam with little bream and catfish.

Under the Searchlight of a Robot Sub

Where the whale lay
on the floor of the canyon
hagfish came to feed in the dark
with shrimp and crab and sea pig.
Boneworms sent roots
into the whale oil
at the core of the bone.
Plumes grew,
microscopic mates inside them
shedding sperm over the eggs
which drifted nowhere
by ten thousands, settling,
some of them, onto another
whale fall miles away.

Inside a ship
with decks lit by the sun,
in the dim light
of a control room,
human brains in bone casements,
male and female, watched
the plumes pink
in the glow of their screens.
They watched—excitedly
scuttling over the keyboards,
tipping the joysticks,
with their delicate,
pink-palmed, flexible hands.

The Loving Essence of the Duckmole

Ornithorhynchus anatinus, a.k.a. tambreet,
mallagong, & boonaburra

The jimmialong, tail plump with fat,
electrosensors tingling in his bill,
the swivel in his hips more like
the bearded dragon's than like mine,
his four-tipped penis at the ready,
is not cute. He is himself. In courtship
having dug two tunnels, his and hers,
which she can close to lay and tend
their clutch of leathery, soft eggs,
by night he swims and sweeps
his bill where muck sparks everywhere
with insect larvae, worms, and crayfish
which the local crayfishers call yabbies.

A puppy-like, warm-blooded
duck-in-a-fur-coat seems, much
as Ronald Reagan's smile, or Bundy's
good-boy grooming, to suggest
what looks innocuous will do no harm.

But in the mating season he secretes from glands
in his hindquarters into the hollow spurs of bone
at either ankle venom so refined that
when a fisherman, let's not say poacher,
tries removing him from a net,
the stab of pain into the man's wrist

bathes him to the shoulder all at once
in fire. The burning arm throbs
everywhere. It swells. The man
in a delirium of pain falls vomiting.
For three days, arm twice normal size,
he writhes, and morphine does not quell
the pain. People stung may think themselves
the ones attacked, although the platypus
in the encounter often dies, the person never.

Observations from a Hillside Stairway on the Day of Atonement, Just Before My Wife and Daughters Break Their Fast

Under the hanging lights in a pool hall
at nineteen I read the table after the break
and followed a map in my head
to take beer money from older men
while, eight thousand miles under my feet,
boys I knew from high school,
some of them, learned to pray.
Now, at a table in Vegas,
holding maybe a rag and an ace,
my son is reading a voice, a glance,
and running probabilities
in his head. Sons of other men
are bivouacked at dawn in a desert
where Abraham's father worshipped
Babylonian gods. Everything wobbles
and spins. Here, in the little woods
a block from Erwin Methodist Church,
bottles drunken boys have shattered
over the brick steps flash
in wobbling streaks of sunlight.
Two hundred years ago, James Erwin
at the end of boyhood left his father's house,
and walked into the local wilderness
to preach. Wolves appeared at dusk,
and the boy with a Bible sang.
He shouted God's praise into the sky.

Here, the fox grapes hang from a guy wire
over the edge of the trees where a doe
and two fawns stand in poison ivy
to the hip. I never did learn
to pray or carry a tune, but I say
these words into my cupped palm
quietly, not to spook the deer.

Kropotkin and the Lake on Mars

Kropotkin worked by the flicker of a tiny oil lamp . . .
During the short hours of the day he would transcribe his
notes on a typewriter . . . Much of his leisure he spent
at the piano.
—EMMA GOLDMAN, JANUARY 1921

Pyotr Kropotkin, scientist of anarchy,
once theorized that the weight of a glacier
must melt ice underneath it into a lake.
Fifty years after Kropotkin died, radar
showed at Vostok Station in the Antarctic
under a glacier two miles thick
one of the largest lakes on Earth.
Now they have found a smaller
such lake under the ice on Mars,
water, saltier than the Dead Sea.
After forty years in exile, and a few
in prison, Kropotkin came home
to a cottage he shared with his wife.
There, in conscience, he wrote
that taking hostages for the revolution
was wrong. When company came, watched
by the secret police, he would play
transcriptions from the Italian opera
so that his musical friends could sing.

Thanks to the Makers of Shells

Factory workers before I was born
　　cut and fitted eighteen pieces of oak wood
to construct the chair at my desk
　　where I have seated myself,
as a hermit-crab-tail might slip into the vacant shell of a conch.

　　Here I let my mind walk sideways,
fingertips tapping the keyboard in my lap more feelingly
　　because each outer shell of a fingernail holds
　　　　the tingling pad alert
　　　　around its inner shell of bone.

　　My laptop closes on its hinge,
the way the operculum of a twisted necklace snail might
　　pull shut at the approach of the hermit crab,
the spool of words, like the snail, enveloped then
　　　　in the nacreousness in the dark.

　　Inside my skull another operculum covers
　　　　the insular lobe
　　where consciousness takes place, as if the mind
were a shell for the flesh, or flesh were a husk
　　　　for the cosmic one.

Message, 1944

In Budapest, after the cherry blossoms fell,
a colonel in the SS asked a leader
from the underground
to carry a message abroad: the SS
would release one million Jews
in exchange for ten thousand trucks
and a thousand tons of tea, coffee, cocoa,
and soap for soldiers on the Russian front.

"Blood for goods," he called the exchange.
Then he inverted the phrase
for effect, "goods for blood."

Almost no one herded onto the trains in Budapest
knew what the leaders of the resistance knew.
In June, on a typical day at Auschwitz, more
Jews died than soldiers in both armies fell
in Normandy on D-Day, which was the sixth.

On the seventh, British intelligence met
the Hungarian messenger's train at Aleppo.
He was trying to help his people, they thought,
but the German offer had to be a trick.

From Aleppo the British took him
to Cairo where they questioned him
for four months. The diplomat
in charge of refugees asked,

"What shall I do with those million
Jews? Where shall I put them?"

The British thought the exchange
of blood for goods would be
collusion against their ally Russia.
Transports of prisoners might be
deployed as human shields for the enemy.
Confusion, involving the demand
for medicine, shelter, and food,
would prolong the end of the war
and undermine negotiations to follow.

Churchill declined the offer. Experts,
some of them, thought that the murder
of Jews, exaggerated in propaganda,
was already reaching an end.

From mid-May into mid-July,
in fact, the SS murdered four hundred
thousand more Hungarian Jews,
more than the total number of American
soldiers killed from the beginning
until the end of the war.

The messenger upon release
joined the resistance in Palestine,
and fought to overthrow British rule.

Later, secret police from Israel kidnapped
the German colonel near his house
in Argentina and brought him
to Jerusalem for trial. He pleaded
innocent. Found guilty, he was put
to death by hanging, this in a prison
near where eyeless scorpions
live in limestone caves.

The messenger believed at the end
of his life that the British assessment
of "blood for goods" was correct.
He regretted his part in the offer.

Blut gegen Ware, at any rate, still
describes the logic of money and war.

Unlit Kitchen, 5 A.M.

After the rain
an old man saw
through the spider web
on a fogged window
far down under the cedars
a cloud on the pond
lift into the daylight.

To Floyd, Louisiana

ca. 1807–ca. 1918

In the Second Great Awakening
Moses Floyd, a Methodist preacher,
came from Pennsylvania
to the swamp, and a few years later
here you were, a town with a dry goods store,
a church, a courthouse, and saloons.

Young men staggered into the dusty street
where guns were a kind of law,
like the hanging tree, and the documents
stating who owned what and whom.

But the steamboats quit their run
on the bayou, and the railroad
and the highway left you, church
and courthouse, store, saloons, and all,
abandoned. Buildings downtown
disappeared. Now there's only a crook
in the two-lane through the level
corn and cotton fields slowly
giving up your name to oblivion,

like the forgotten name of the mounds
nearby on Bayou Macon, where the people
who gathered hickory nuts, persimmons,
scuppernongs, and mayhaws, cast
their weighted nets for catfish, cooked

in covered pits, using ceramic stones
to set the heat. One of them carved
a bannerstone in the shape of wings,
another made a throwing stick for a spear,
and all of them died three thousand years ago.

A few days' walk southwest
is another circle of mounds, these
from before the reign of Gilgamesh.
The people who built them
fished for the drum which Frenchmen
taught me as a boy to call the gaspergou.

Near there, Floyd, when you were young,
children huddled among their elders
on a steamboat called the *Cleopatra*.
On a river through deep woods
sheathed in ice they were passing
into another world, taken by strangers
out of the only world they knew
in a kind of boat that trembled
with a guttural moan. And near you,
Floyd, under trees far larger
than any alive now in that region,
another party of Choctaw came on foot,
young men, old men, women, and children
following lost guides in the swamp where limbs
snapped under the weight of ice and toppled.

Sunset, Mare Spumans

The dust on the floor
of the Foaming Sea
is barren in all directions.
One last spark at the uppermost
limb of the Sun blinks out
into a seemingly
infinite swarm of stars,
and the dust cools
in the next Earth day
from the boiling point
of water down to the freezing
point of gasoline.

From the Journal of Dr. Beaurieux

*Witness to an execution by guillotine,
June 28, 1905*

After the blade dropped, and the eyelids twitched,
the spasms tugging at the lips went calm,
and when I called out to the head, "Languille!"
the eyelids lifted up, this time, I swear,
in a distinctly normal movement, slow,
as if awakening, or torn from thought.
With pupils focusing themselves, the eyes
looked sharp, not like a dying man's, not vague,
and when the lids went shut, I called again,
"Languille!" and again, without a twitch,
they lifted, and the eyes looked into mine.

To the Water Bear

Kleiner Wasserbär, observed by Pastor Johann Goeze,
Quedlinburg, December 10, 1772

Jesus in his little boat said to the crowd
on the bank at Galilee
that the mustard seed, the smallest of all seeds,
is to the full-grown tree
as our mere inkling of the kingdom of heaven is
to the kingdom itself.

Maybe the mustard seed is not the smallest
of all seeds and does not really grow
into a tree. The point was not to measure
seeds, or where we go after we die. The point
was reckoning beyond measure.

You, of course, were small,
much smaller than the mustard seed.
Yet to the German pastor who first saw you
move as if in slow-mo underwater,
under the microscope, you looked
enormous, eight stout legs, he called them feet,
with claws like those of a brown bear:
water bear, he called you . . . little water bear.

Your mouth was something else,
a nozzle for a telescoping vacuum
set with teeth. It struck, and drew the prey
back onto the twin blades inside for the kill.

Gentlemen in those days used
the hunting rifle, which was the latest thing,
to slaughter every bear in every patch of woods
in their whole country, so that the first
brown bear at large in Germany
since Bismarck came of age was famous
just ten years ago. Bruno,
they called him. From the Italian Alps
he walked for weeks through Austria
into the borderland where Germans shot
their last wild bear in eighteen thirty-five.
He celebrated this return by killing
thirty sheep, assorted goats, chickens,
rabbits, and one little girl's pet guinea pig,
which he finished chewing
on the front stoop of the *Polizei*.

Tourists at the local inns, grown fearful
that he might kill some of them, soon
had him shot, stuffed, and set up on display
nearby in their Museum of Mankind and Nature.

Living, you would not have recognized
your likeness in the body of your cousin
Bruno. You lacked optics in your eye spots
and your brain had too few cells. In death,
however, limitations of the living fall away,

or that, at least, would seem to be the premise
of my speaking to you in this poem.

You water bears, unlike your cousins,
thrive in Germany, and everywhere,
from lichens on Antarctic mountainsides
and moss along the Nile down
into the silt bed of the Coral Sea.
You can withstand extremes of heat
and cold. Irradiated, poisoned,
under crushing depths of pressure, or sent
floating into the void of outer space, you live.
Though dried-out, crumpled in a heap like duck cloth,
still, when watered, you can twitch, and come to life.
Your species has survived five hundred million years.

Just after the German, an Italian cleric
with a microscope gave you the name
from Latin tardigrade, slow stepper,
like what *Beowulf* calls the monster
Grendel: *mearcstapa*, boundary
stepper. That's you too. It's Bruno,
me, and every living thing, all teetering
along the edge. And look! I like the way
you move out here. To my mind, you
surpass the kingdom of heaven: you exist.

The Nationality of Neptune

The planet seafaring people call
Poseidon in the Cyclades,
speakers of one local tongue
in Veracruz call Tlaloc,
after their god of bodies
of water, storms, fertility,
and of the realm of the dead.
To delight Tlaloc Aztecs
used to dress the children
of captives and of the chosen
nobles in colorful paper smocks,
with feathers and shells.
On ceremonial mountaintops
and in caves, high priests
with obsidian knife blades
opened the children to remove
their living hearts. Their screams
and tears, some said, brought down
the blessing of rain. Others
chosen of that god they buried
with foreheads painted blue and seeds
placed on their faces. The planet
Tlaloc is not visible to the naked eye.

The Arctic Vortex at Snooks Pond, 2014

The warmest groundwater seeping into the marsh
before it froze for the first time smoked, and ice flowers
formed in the smoke. Ice petals radiated from low twigs.
Ice feathers hung from the willow trunk reflected.
Spurs took shape on the black sheen just now frozen.
Farther out on the pond, in the deep snow, powder
sifted into cracks where the old ice was contracting
with a chirp like sonar. Cracks in the snow gaped, wide
as an old man's knuckle, crisscross, so that the pond
was a white mosaic, each tile big as a dance floor.
Tracks from a fox, and from deer and rabbits, marked
the dance steps. A man at the sight of the cracked ice,
though he knew better, felt as if he might fall through.
But the clear ice under the cracks held. It was like him.

Apologies to the Dead

1. TO RUTH STEIN BLUM
1866–1929

Passenger pigeons came
rivering endlessly
into your childhood,
and when you were grown
the last one, Martha,
lived on display
at the Cincinnati Zoo.
She was brown and buff
and dull gray, only her eyes
bright orange, each
with a pale blue ring.

2. TO MARY DEFRANCE
1848–1902

The census before the War has you, age fifteen,
living with a physician, thirty-five. At Shiloh
he was a surgeon with the Fourth Infantry
from Louisiana. The Union advanced,
and you fled home for Vicksburg
where the Fourth Infantry fought again.
When the smell of the rotting dead
and screams from the cracked throats
of the wounded forced both sides
to call a three-hour truce, boys

about to kill each other talked
and traded in a calm between-time
while they tended their friends.
You must have been waiting then
in one of the dirt caves under the bluff,
where people went with carpets, tables,
chairs, and beds, to weather the shelling
from Admiral Porter's boats. Your new
husband, George Fontaine, was one of the boys
who surrendered. Later, the two of you opened
a dry-goods store in Floyd. Near there
the surgeon, who must have been your father,
murdered an immigrant in cold blood.

3. TO DR. WALTER L. DEFRANCE
1822–?

When the Lord God bird still nested in the swamp,
at three in the afternoon, there was a warm rain.
It was Monday, the first of July, eighteen
sixty-seven. A knock came at the front door.
Herman Stein, my great-great-grandfather,
answered, and you, whose name was never
mentioned in this story, witnessed by his wife
and three small children, drew a pistol . . .
you, as a gentleman, having taken offense
when billed for your delinquent debt by a Jew.

My father, Kenneth, told me the story told him
by his grandmother, Ruth, who was there
as a toddler when her father died. You,
she said, having shot him in cold blood, went
unpunished, never charged with a crime.
Lately, however, I find that you did not
shoot my kinsman in cold blood.

Newspapers report: it was a stabbing.
The Times-Picayune includes with other
news from the region one short paragraph
on the murder. This comes after a farmer's
complaint that steady rains have made grass
grow up over his cotton. In the mud, he says,
the freedmen cannot plow. The next paragraph
reports the murder, noting that any one
of the nine stab wounds would have been fatal.
Another farmer says that his corn is healthy,
but that worms may yet develop. In *The Daily
Memphis Avalanche* a quote from *The Carroll
Record* states that you were "legally arrested";
but, "to the surprise and disappointment of all,"
you made your escape.

                    That night would have been
cloudy with no moon. In the unusual darkness,
it would seem, you found that you could evade

your captors. Something of this kind kept happening
in Louisiana. Of white men who had committed
that year more than two hundred illegal shootings,
stabbings, hangings, whippings, and beatings
of the legally free, not one was charged with a crime.

The newspapers' mention of *legal* arrest in this case
makes it appear that stabbing a Jew nine times
at his home in front of his wife and children might
be thought unacceptable.

                    No further record exists
of you as Dr. DeFrance, except your expulsion
the following year from the Masonic Lodge.

The census from eighteen fifty listed you
as a farmer, head of household, Laura, your wife,
baby Ada, and Mary, then two years of age.
This was in Mississippi. In Louisiana,
as *Doctor* DeFrance, you were three years younger
than the farmer would be, and lived alone
with Mary, three years older than the farmer's child.

Why would someone have made the two of you
on record six years closer in age, and how
might this bear on the savagery of the murder?
Who invented the story about the bill and the handgun?

What rage, Walter, drove you there,
to the front door, out of your mind, with a knife?

4. TO MARY TERRELL HOWARD SESSIONS DEFRANCE
1775–1833

You must have been one
of the orphans and foundlings
shipped from Europe to be the wives
of men in the colonial South.

After the Revolutionary War,
according to family records, you
at the age of eight gave birth.
Maybe the records are mistaken.

But by the time there was a Bill
of Rights, you had four boys:
Asa, Robert, James, and Frederick.

And you were sixteen. Then your husband,
at the age of thirty-three, seems
to have turned his attention
elsewhere, fathering twins
by another girl, whose name
and age I cannot find.

After your first four boys
were grown, you became

at forty-one the wife
of another man to whom
you bore three sons,
Parke, Walter, and Charles,
you for the last of these past fifty.

Your one girl seems to have died
as a child. You died
when you were fifty-eight.
You were twelve years
dead when Walter named
his first girl Mary after you.

Walter then, in middle age,
stabbed my kinsman
Herman Stein nine times.

I cannot tell you why,
in front of a man's wife
and three children, your boy
Walter would stab and stab
and stab the man, nine times . . .

I cannot say what good
your Walter may have done
with his surgical knife
at Shiloh or at Vicksburg,
in the worst of the battles
where he served . . .

nor what harm he did
before the War, to his wife
who left him, or to his children,
your grandchildren,
Ada and Mary . . . Mary,
whom he gave your name . . .

Flower Medley

after lines by Hayden Carruth, 1921–2008

Before the spasms tore his heart,
before the doctors tethered him
with oxygen, and blinded him, he breathed,
out walking with good friends, a raft
of hyacinth in Brooklyn, and the white bloom
of the blue plum broke. Daylilies came back
in summer with orange tongues of flame.
The sour cherry four years dead
bloomed one morning in October,
and a red hibiscus dropped onto the floor.
Because he put these into poems,
the old geranium still holds ten blossoms.
The moth he called Catocala, or hidden beauty,
frets, and beats the screen. For love
he named them, not just moths, or flowers:
stones, and animals, musicians by the score.
Today the purple shoots of hellebore
have broken through the frozen dirt.
Doctors, he reminded me, once brewed
from hellebore a cure for madness—
he looked up—and it was deadly.
I loved Hayden when he laughed.

Eclipse

August 28, 2007

While the Moon sank into a reef of clouds,
the shadow I had come to see slid down
past craters formed a billion years before
life formed on Earth.

My father at eighty
lost three quarts of blood inside his gut
and buckled in my arms, so that we both
fell at his bedside. On the floor he told me,
eyes relaxing, quiet, No, he would be fine,
please, not to call the ambulance.

From him
when I was twelve I learned to watch the Moon
with his refractor scope, imagining
the surface as a texture human hands
could touch. Now he was gone, and I stood
in a field alone among half-moonlit rocks.

After my mother's sweetheart died in the War,
my father, who had been her college friend,
thought they might make a life. Third
to form in my mother's womb,
on the third day I was a mulberry of cells
suspended in the dark inside her.

In a book of myths she gave me as a child
the god of the Moon in Egypt is a scribe
delivering his wisdom to the dead.

Now one crow flapped though shelves of mist
into the floodlit aura of a mall
beyond the woods, and half in shadow,
half in clouds, the Moon kept sinking.

The Morning Star in Babylon, the book
said, was a goddess toward whom women
cried in childbirth, one who turned
toward men by dawn the cryptic sexual look
in light of which the brave supposedly seek war.

My parents' love misled them into betrayal
and confusion. When my father turned
for comfort toward young men, the way
my mother did for years with women,
she divorced him. I was confused less
by their pain than by the numbing in myself.

Later in middle age my wife tried cursing me
to ask for love, and I withdrew. At my feet,
at the edge of a field now, rocks no longer moonlit
tilted toward the Morning Star in the east.

Near Saturn

Snowflakes drifted unseen
onto the floor of a lake.
Salts of cyanide fell nearby
in the rainfall over the crags.
Other moons appeared
to the instruments of the eye,
some cratered, one smooth, one of them
spouting water crystals into space.
And we could see odd shapes less
moonlike, Epi-metheus and Pro-metheus
meaning After-thought and Fore-thought
shepherding rocks and ice
in the rings. And others, moonlets,
were invisible, smaller, nameless, most,
like most of what there was and is,
even to the mind's eye dark.

Lingerie Femme *and the Vagaries of Pronunciation*

From *vagari*, Latin, meaning *wander*,
comes *vah-GEHR-ee*, an eccentric whim,
or deviation in the fickle mind. Vagaries
are not instances of vagueness, though the new
pronunciation, *VAYG-uh-reez*, has blurred
the meaning. Let's not blur the meaning. *Aks*
for *ask* was standard during the reign
of Aelfric. If a bigot tells you *aks* is wrong,
remind him that King Eadgar and Queen
Aelfthryth disagreed. This error is not
trivial, though to err, Pope said, is human,
and he did say *uhr*, not *ehr*. To air is what
the British do not do with dirty linen.
Flax, speaking of linen, is the proper sound
in *flaccid*, which, like *accident*,
and unlike *acid*, has two cees. *Lingerie*
is French for *linen*. I struggle to accept
(two cees, *ak-sept*) that in this country
lingerie is *lawnjuhray*. It's sad. I love
to mangle French as much as anyone,
and if it made me feel indecent
lawnjuhray would be a triumph,
but it calls to my mind someone
injured in a folding lawn chair.

To Bald Eagle

You were a good workhorse,
gentle for children to ride.
When I leaned forward on your neck
and whispered, I could feel it
that you understood me.
Even in your old age Henry Davis
would have you prance, and he swung down
from the height of your back, easy
out of the saddle when he was eighty.
The mule that shared your stall
for years, Henry told us after he hauled
your body away from the house,
stood screaming over what was left,
for three days. Then, for a few more seasons,
Henry ploughed his cornfield with the mule.
Now, fifty years later, I'm whispering this to myself.

Circa 1961

Titanis walleri

A flightless raven taller than a man
kept chasing me into the ditch along the road.
Nightmare logic made the bird too slow
ever to catch me, but it also made me
stumble. Sea cows, hundreds of miles southeast,
slipped, meanwhile, through clear springs
into the tea-brown tannic brew
of the Lower Santa Fe, a river
famous for disappearing underground
and coming up out of nowhere. There,
in scuba gear, Ben Waller did
palaeoarchaeology for fun. He sank
his bare hands into the silt on bottom
to feel his way along for hidden shapes.
He found whole points of pre-Columbian spears,
and once the fossilized ankle
of the most frightening bird
ever to walk this Earth.
Waller's job for Civil Defense
was diving to bring back bodies of divers
lost in local caves. The anklebone
he found was what they call
Titanis walleri, a bird the size of the one
in my contemporaneous nightmare.
Two million years before,
that species may have made the laugh
the seriema makes now in Brazil.

The seriema can catch a snake in her beak,
whip it into the ground,
and swallow it whole, head first.
With a similar motion, they say,
Titanis, to protect her chicks,
could bring down cats as big as tigers.
She did this by driving her beak
hook first into the cat's spine—
head, an eagle's head more massive
than a battle-ax, swung down
by the muscle-bound neck of an emu
twice the size of my father, who was tall,
and, I should tell you, kind,
but who happened to own the black
totemic carving of a crow
which came to life enormous in my dreams.

Oceanic

1.

Again an oriole has hung her nest
among the cottonwoods just
farther north, and soon
inside the Baltimore hotel
where my grandparents stood
as newlyweds big horseshoe crabs
will scuttle over the lobby floor
while high tide laps
through busted
window frames and doors.

2.

When the north wind came down
out of the cedars
onto the bay
the boat turned slowly
as the needle of a compass
does in the palm of a man
turning to find himself
on a map.

3.

Far down, under a sky without a moon or stars,
when the dive light failed and the current

along the wall of the reef gained force,
he turned to find the lights of the others
gone. Things in the total dark, even
his own hands now, seemed hypothetical,
and deep inside the ear the velocity of his heart.

To Sirius B

Your sister, the Dog Star, was the brightest.
You, the Pup, nobody even saw, until one night
in eighteen sixty-two, when a young man
with a telescope of his own devise looked up,
and there, where the wobble in your sister's gait
suggested you might be, you were, a white dwarf.
Scientists, when they could read your temperature,
said a thimbleful of you must weigh a ton.
Fusion had to have ceased, they thought,
for you to be so dense. Though white hot
you were defunct at the core, already yellowing,
dead in other words. After the yellow,
they predicted, would come dull red, duller
and duller, until you disappeared. Your sister,
meanwhile, and the Sun would also be white
dwarves. Mercury, Venus, Earth, and the Moon,
before that, during the Sun's red-giant phase,
would have been vaporized in the expanding
sphere and thrown off into nebulous plumes.

A Voter from Mississippi Considers
the State Constitution

Article 12, Section 241 on Franchise:
Concerning the Exception for Idiots and Insane Persons

Words ring empty without love,
but we do in the strictest sense
rank *idiots* below the *imbeciles*
and *imbeciles* below the *morons*.
Idiots we deem unfit to vote.
This is the law. In May of 1954,
soon after *Brown vs. Board of Education*,
Senator James Eastland in his third term
said that segregation is the law
of nature. It keeps racial harmony,
he said. His people a year later
murdered Emmett Till.
During his fourth term they killed
Evers, Chaney, Schwerner, and Goodman.
During his fifth, nearby in Tennessee,
they murdered King. Those deemed
worthy of the vote made Eastland senator
six times. When Eastland was a boy
they made James Vardaman
their governor, then senator.
Vardaman in his first campaign
for governor said education spoiled
good field hands, and he advocated
lynching. Our state constitution

for a time required that voters
demonstrate sound moral character.
That statute was repealed.

A Cat Lover's Guide to The Bell Curve

Pigs may be the most intelligent
of the domestic animals,
but next to pigs cats look like
geniuses for diet, caterwauling
sex, longevity, and hygiene.
Sows suffocate their young
by accident, or swallow them
alive on whim. I've seen them
puke their breakfast in the dirt
and eat it warm for lunch, their faces
smeared with shit. The poor,
some experts say, are less intelligent
than the rich. This they prove
with numbers from a test
which, I'm just guessing,
is the one they use on pigs.

To Jesse James

Before you were born, your father stood
in the pulpit quoting the gospel:
"As ye would that men should do
to you, do ye also to them
likewise." He kept five children:
to work as slaves in the hemp fields,
and their mother in the house.

When you were three, he left
for Hangtown Gold Camp
where he found what many young men
found there, cholera and an early death.

Your stepfather beat you, and your mother
replaced him soon with the Doctor,
who worked the children to raise tobacco.

Your brother Frank, having left home
at eighteen, was asleep in the Rebel camp
at dawn, when boys from the Union
crept up through the woods,
and the Battle of Wilson's Creek
left five hundred dead around him.
In the siege at Lexington he surrendered.
Home on parole he joined a Rebel gang.

Then, you saw jayhawkers hang the Doctor
from a tree in the yard. They swung him

down to ask where Frank had gone,
and when he did not say, they swung him up again.

A year later, Frank came back with Bloody Bill's gang,
and you joined them at sixteen to murder
the unarmed boys on the train at Centralia.
The Union infantry followed and took a position
with muskets, to pour and pack and fire
as fast as they could, but you and the gang of boys
on horseback charged with two or three revolvers each,
killing a hundred more, including some who surrendered.

You were an outlaw then for life.
You received at your work
two bullet wounds in the chest
and one in the leg.

When you were thirty-four, you, your wife, and children
shared a house with the Ford boys: Robert,
after breakfast, shot you in the back of the head,
having been promised more than he thought
to earn in a lifetime, more, in fact, than he did.

Some say, you were an excellent dancer,
courteous with the ladies. Stories tell
of your saving a widow's farm.
They mention widows in several states.

I keep trying to see the actual man
behind the eyes in the photograph:
hair and beard cut short, jacket tweed
with a clover lapel, floppy silk bow tie:
a man of moderate style, alert to trouble
such as upholders of slavery met
in the Borderlands of your time.

Frank I see here bald at fifty-five,
big ears, turn-of-the-century three-piece suit
and sweater, wingtip collar and flowing tie,
more shoe salesman by now than robber:
Frank looks less on edge, having killed more
boys and men by far than you did.

When he returned to the farm in old age,
after your mother died, for two bits
he would show the original site of your grave
and let the visitor take a pebble
to keep as a souvenir.

There's no connection between us, Jesse,
except the enjoyment of lives prepared by those
who made their neighbors slaves under color of law
and by armies deployed at a whim.

In the predawn dark while my mother
was giving birth to me, your namesake Jesse,

six when last you saw him at the table for breakfast,
would have been sleeping, an old man
in Los Angeles, in South Central where he lived.

He died there too, the following year, eight miles south
of where my brother Richard lives today.

Love and Empire

Napoleon in exile kept two lockets, one
from the late Marie Walewska
with a snippet of blonde hair, the other
remembering Josephine with violets
he picked beside her grave. As for himself,
he asked that his heart in spirits of wine,
preserved in a dish of silver welded
shut, be given to the second
empress, who survived him.

*

Widowed at thirty, jailed
by Robespierre, made
courtesan by his successor,
Josephine, when she laughed, hid
her ugly teeth behind her hand.

*

Napoleon two days after the wedding left for war.
He said in a letter to his wife, he longed to kiss
her breast, "and lower down, much lower." Her replies
were cool and few; her dalliances with his rival, not.

*

Sick of his wife's adulteries, Napoleon in Egypt
saw a woman smiling with good teeth
and sent her husband as envoy to France.
The smiling woman stayed, and with the wives

of other officers she visited the general's house
for lunch. A parlormaid filling the water glasses
tripped and drenched the woman's dress.
Napoleon, as though surprised, leapt up,
and led his guest into a private room where,
he insisted, she could "repair the damage."

*

Marie Walewska, faithful as a wife
at twenty-one, according to her own
account, had spurned Napoleon.
But when he smashed his watch,
and swore that he would shatter
Poland, thus, were she not his,
she fainted, wakening after the rape
to find him soothing her, as if in love.

*

Men who saw bells fat as oxen
drop through bell towers in flames
after a month lay scattered, windblown
in a thousand fields of snow.

*

Marie Walewska spent two nights in Napoleon's bed
on Elba, planning to stay, but he escorted her
on the third night halfway back to the boat.

In the locket she had inscribed: "Remember,
when you cease to love me, that I love you still."

*

The perfume of the violet is sweet, though brief
because it numbs the nerve it touches.

*

Declining the gift of the dead man's heart,
the second empress wrote to a friend:
"He did not treat me ill, as some
suppose. I would have wished him
many years of a contented life,
if only he lived them far away from me."

From Anyte of Tegea

For you, goddess of war and wisdom,
I leave this cherrywood pike
three times the length of my body.

I have wiped from the iron leaf
the blood of men
whose lives I ended.

Soon my name and the names
of victorious kings
and kingdoms will be nothing.

Still, in the light of your
mind, goddess, may
the brave soul glimmer.

The Cormorant at Snooks Pond

After the mall tycoon paid experts to conclude
that rainbow trout can survive in water like this,
warm and rich from a wetlands, three years
after they drained the pond, and excavators
had sunk the bottom deep enough to please him,
when masons had dressed the face of the levee
for show with a stone wall high as a two-story house,
when the water rose, and the fishery stocked it
with yearlings in good health, a few days later,
the trout were already slow, and a cormorant came
to fish beside the dam. The mall tycoon keeps
weakening with age, and now his trout are failing him.
But the dam he built will outlast everyone living.

Bananas

A monkey with the muttonchops and lips
of Henrik Ibsen barked, and creatures
on the forest floor stood still to sniff
and listen. There, a traveler might pick,
according to Jules Verne, a fruit "healthy
as bread and succulent as cream." Buddha
ate bananas in that realm. And Jesus
would have loved them, if he lived nearby,
or later. Muhammad with his wisdom
brought about the great diffusion of bananas
west, into the Andalusian caliphate where Berbers
ate black figs. Experts say, *banana*, Spanish,
comes from Portuguese, from Wolof
slave merchants who got it from the Berbers'
Arabic, *banaana*, meaning *finger*. They
don't know. Fine tailors made kimonos
for the summer heat from fabric woven
of the softest, innermost banana leaf. Bashō
wore *bashofu*, one student says, and wrote
while kneeling on a carpet of banana silk.
After United Fruit made sweet bananas
cheap and plentiful, former rabbi Eli Black
acquired the company and paid his workers,
in good conscience, six times more,
but when the company, and then his conscience,
and then bribes and tax schemes, failed,
he took his briefcase, bashed the window

from an office forty-four floors up,
and threw his papers and himself
out of the New York skyline into the street.

The Moons of Jupiter

My wife and I looked after they found one
about the size of Hawaii, and a smaller one
shaped like a russet potato with craters
for eyes, not that we saw them. What we saw
was the neighborhood where we lived, lit
by streetlights in the rain. My wife said
Patsy Cline had fallen out of a sky like that
in Tennessee years earlier. A pilot
with too little training thought he could fly her
home in a storm. Jupiter has one old storm
about the size of Alaska, and seventy-nine moons,
most with a surface area less than that of the state
park in Topanga Canyon. Two of the four moons
Galileo saw have crusts of ice with oceans
underneath. Mountain lions live in Topanga
Canyon, *inside* the city limits of LA. Unusual
salamanders live there too. Nobody knows
what lives in the ocean under the ice
on Europa. Nothing would be my guess.

Don't Get Me Wrong

In praise of George Starbuck
and his poem "Of Late"

My younger colleague told me, when I praised the poem
of a dead white man, that this was microaggression.
I tried to explain that the poem protested aggression too,
during the war in Vietnam. By bashing McNamara,
then the secretary of defense, the poem advocated peace.
My colleague said he advocated peace by bashing me.
Differences in scale and point of view may be deceptive.
Gamma rays, for example, with a wavelength of one
micromicron, leave an infinitesimal fleck in photographs
of space where a star far larger than most exploded
light-years from the Milky Way. The Milky Way
from out there is another fleck, adrift in the limitless
dark with galaxies flung in all directions, each
at its core having crushed into a pinhole several
million times the mass of the Sun. When power
bears down, things get full of themselves sometimes
and send out bad vibes everywhere. One gamma burst
nearby, according to professors in Kansas, killed
most living things on Earth. But that was before
what we call consciousness, when living things
were small, and nobody cared. Lately, hydrogen
bombs make bad vibes too, and the atoms
are only a few gamma wavelengths across.
The poem about the war maintains that dropping
napalm on an innocent civilian is no less wrong
when you call your target the enemy aggressor.

My colleague and I agree. What we've got here,
Cool Hand Luke reminded the Walking Boss
(who promptly shot him dead), is a failure
to communicate. The poem blames smug
white men for bombing people said to be less
white, though it doesn't mention gender or the color
of anyone's skin. I met the poet in an elevator
when I was a mailboy where he taught, and his skin
had that pink tone of Angora cat lips, slightly muted.
The dazzle in his mind, prodigious then, is gone.
But poems of his, if you care to read them, come alive.

Tracks Everywhere at Noon

Where a bobcat leapt across the vanishing
rafter of prints from a turkey tom
with jakes and hens, to look
at the tracks and picture the animals
in the act of leaving them took me
out of myself as a boy, the way it did
to walk out waist deep into the River.

Hidden in all that water from woods
and fields in thirty states one drop,
I was thinking, might have melted weeks back
under a marmot asleep on the ice
near Three Forks, and that one drop might
in another month glide over the blacktip fin
of a shark downstream across the Gulf.

Almost everything was hidden: eels
in the cool dark underwater at noon
with spoonbill catfish, and snapping turtles
bigger and older than I would ever be.

Behind the blue there had to be planets,
thousands, with living creatures I could never
imagine, and clusters of stars afloat on the surge
of nothing out of nowhere. The current
where I stood in the full noon sun felt cool
on my legs and hands, a mile wide,
moving steadily as the River of Heaven,

which (fifty years later) landed me *here*
on the solid ice of a big pond with a dog
we brought home cowering from the pound.

So here she went now, after a few months free
from harm, galloping into the blizzard at noon,
springing into the drifts, beside herself to smell
tracks everywhere, crisscross, filled with snow.

The Bewilderment

My friend in high school said, God
love her, Yes, and there was nookie,
and we saw that it was good. And lay
bewildered on a sandbar which the River
washed into the Gulf. And in her brother's
treehouse, which was broken, as were we.

We said goodbye, and in another world
I walked out onto the rubble of Our Lady
of the Caves and Beasts in Ephesus.
Where a patchwork column stands
I stood. And dreamed. And met a college girl
with whom I shared hashish, and crabs.
She wanted to be the one on top, and it was
nookie prelapsarian as light in heaven.

Later, in the Rust Belt, in a heat wave,
God's apocalyptic messenger downtown
kept shouting: Torment is eternal
and the Lake of Fire awaits. I looked him
in the eye and fell through helpless.
But my friend in vinyl platform pumps
with six-inch heels reached after me.
She took me by the hand, and led me home.

According to a book my father gave me,
nookie names a woman's tender part
or person with "a kind of baby talk . . .

almost polite," and in more recent use
it names the love between two men,
the tenderness that follows after a kiss,
a touch, a nibble in the kitchen while we cook,
an act which state laws meltingly approve.

As did my father, and as Jesus must have done
at supper, when he took John to his bosom.
Also John, who wrote this. And the John
who said in First John, "God is
love." And Wild John, I would guess,
who ate his locusts dipped in honey
and felt glad to hear the Bridegroom's voice.

But as for the John who said that locusts
sting like scorpions, so that the men stung
writhe in pain for days until they seek
the balm of death, though death flees,
and the men for five months pine away,
they fall in their bewilderment,
and in the dust they see the stinging
locusts with thoraxes like torsos
of blood horses dressed for battle,
and with gold crowns on their heads,
their faces like men's faces,
but with women's hair, and teeth
the teeth of lions: John, alone on Patmos,
saw this: he was pining for God's love.

To the Moon

After I thumbed a ride I saw you
in the passenger window, more
than a crescent, almost half.
It was getting dark, and a voice
on the car radio was reporting
that Neil Armstrong had stepped
onto the Sea of Tranquility.
He was walking there in the dust.

Five times more, men visited,
two at a time. Some of them
lowered Moon buggies out of a bay
in the side of the lander. These
they unfolded and took for a spin.

Flower children of my generation
thought that the men were middle-aged,
and they were, but they were children too.
They left Moon buggies in your lap.

I wanted to tell you last year,
when I saw you in the bare limbs
at your narrowest crescent
next to the Morning Star,
and just this fall when you were large
and bright as I had ever seen:

to consider you in the night sky is
to release the mind more deeply into itself.

If Earth is alive, you were alive
when these men lived on you.
When they left you died,
and they plunged living into the sea.

Transit of Venus, 1882

Known for unruly auburn hair
and a dark look and the moody
talk only his sister took to heart,
he felt urgency was a virtue.

But when he proposed to his sister's friend,
she wanted him to join the church,
and after he settled into the practice of law,
finally, when she said *I do*, what he wanted
on their wedding night went nowhere.

＊

A junco nesting just outside flew
at her own reflection, skull first
thumping into the glass,
over and over every day.

The lady of the house made plans
for a luncheon and for whist.

The counselor walked for miles
in the woods around the lake.
She had not wanted him,
she did not, and she never would.

＊

More and more in the face of his wife
at fifty, entertaining guests,

he saw the smile of her father
the barkeep, dead from drink.

A young astronomer told their friends
scattering light waves in thin air
tinted the clear sky blue.

    *

The counselor's son at twenty
taught the astronomer's wife a step
they called the Hesitation Waltz. He let it be
known he found her irresistible as a flirt,
and dance lessons ended in a parting of ways.

    *

But the counselor, who was her father's age,
kept taking her on carriage rides in the country.

He brought her to play and sing for his sisters,
the way she learned at the Conservatory in Boston.
The sisters, both of them single, pitied him
in his marriage, and after she sang they let him know
they approved . . . though one of them
listened only from her room upstairs.

The following day he spoke as he said he must,
pausing outside the gate, and he saw, when he spoke,
she hesitated before she looked away.

*

Within a month her husband had left
on an expedition to California
where he wrote in his diary
about the transit of Venus photographed
from an observatory on the Pacific,
"We saw things as plain as was ever seen
with any glass in the world."

His wife, meanwhile, explored
the December woods near home
in the company of the older man.

*

Within a year the counselor's youngest,
eight years old, contracted a fever. This
was the boy who had returned his father's
affection always, often it seemed
when there was no one else.

*

Having buried his son, he lay in bed
with malaria for a week, shivering, sweating,
begging forgiveness from the dead.

When he appeared again in public
he wore the wig he had worn for years,

with the unruly auburn hair of his youth,
but under the pallor of illness and age
in his face there was a wound past healing.

※

The astronomer and his wife
decided together, it was time:
she took the older man as her lover
now in the elegant dining room
of the house where he was born,
his wife asleep in the house next door,
the sisters quiet in their beds upstairs.

※

For years to come, after observing the stars,
the husband home at daybreak
would whistle a tune from a comic opera
to let the lovers know he had arrived.

※

The astronomer's wife had forgiven him
his affairs, not that he would ever change
or repent. But he came home. He built
a fire. He laid out pillows by the hearth.
He led her there, and knelt,
and spoke while he undressed her.

※

At first, to relieve the uneasiness in her mind
she needed devotion from her husband.
And later, more, from her lover. She needed
to search the tenderness in their hands,
their mouths, the urgency in the face of one,
and then of the other, often that same day.
The two men, meanwhile, had become good friends.

 *

Because the dance lessons ended in a parting of ways,
the eldest reported everything to his mother.
It was a secret everyone everywhere knew.
Her sisters-in-law had known
in advance. The congregation
knew, faculty, faculty wives.
Her neighbors' servants knew.
Shopkeepers. Judges. Deans.

 *

In the year of mourning for their son
endless arguments led nowhere.
He was a man of the law. Pleading,
with him, was even more useless than tears.

When she suggested renovating the house,
and he objected to the expense, she wheeled
to rip at the wallpaper with her hands.
When she threw a kitchen knife

at his heart, what surprised her
least was her revulsion,
seeing him walk away.

*

Her well-known evenings now
became a travesty for gawkers.
She, the unloved wife, must
drunkenly play herself.

*

For years, even on days he planned
to spend the night in his neighbor's arms,
he wrote love letters she believed immortal.
My gate to God, she called him, and *my King*.

*

The astronomer after the death of his friend
groped his daughter's college classmates.
Having been among the first to see
the Martian moons, in his sixties
he was asked to retire, suffering by then
from violent fits of madness.
These persisted after the death
of his wife into extreme old age.
His scientific project in his decline
was a formula for eternal youth.

*

A painter of exotic birds and flowers
took the astronomer's wife
as his pupil when she was young.
She painted for the reclusive sister
the Indian pipe in bloom.

The sister said in her thank-you note,
though some called this the ghost
plant, it had always been for her
"the preferred flower of life."

They found in the upstairs room
hundreds of original poems. These
the younger woman worked for years
to edit and publish in three books,
embossed in gold on the cover of each
an image of the Indian pipe.

Qoheleth

I used to think the Preacher meant by *vanity*
the sin of pride, but it was *emptiness*.
He said, *Emptiness of emptinesses*.
All is emptiness. Third from the last verse
of his little book is a note to himself and us:
"Of making many books there is no end."

Where But to Think Is to Be Full of Sorrow

In the Bardo of Becoming, reequipped with all five senses
after death, the soul must struggle to accept a vision
of its future life.

If I came back a mollusk, I believe
that slipping my briny clamhood whole
over the tongue of the one I love
for her to savor my living flesh would be
delicious, even without the brain to tell myself
how she might feel. I doubt, meanwhile, that having
a beak in the folds of my crotch, a scrotum
for a head, warts, bulging eyes, and snakelike
arms arrayed with suction cups for clinging
will arouse even the loneliest snorkler at the reef.
Still, I would rather yearn, and be an octopus,
than die more happily inside her as a clam.
Just to change my color from bruised plum
to peach and in a second jonquil streaked
with oxblood and sky blue, to my mind, looks
voluptuous—to his . . . is his a mind? . . . who knows?
He can see, experts say, quite well, two
optic fields at once, though not in color,
polarized. He sees, beyond the brain's ability
to prompt or follow, movements of his own
arms imitating body language from more deadly
species such as lionfish and snakes.
When I pretended to know a book
I had not read, I watched myself like that:

the way a prowler on a starlit reef
might watch his arms taste what they touch
without the brain's consent. We like to think,
as homo sapiens, we choose, and then
we choose in fear to live half numb, half stunned,
not like the octopus in an unlighted
lab at night who eyes fish in the tank
across from his and, though wellfed, conducts
a foray: he slips out under the tank lid,
crawls the length of the counter, climbs sheer glass
into the other tank, consumes the fish,
and crosses home before the lab attendant
comes to work that morning. He can also learn,
they say, to thread a maze, distinguish
geometric shapes, and twist the snug lid
from a jar of crabmeat. I believe, in my next
life, when I unfurl my body out of a seam
between enormous lobes of coral
where I have hidden from a moray eel,
when I jet myself, arms trailing, straight up
into the Moon that floats over the calm
face of the ocean, when my arms have spread
their webbing so that I drift umbrella-like
to mimic the man-o'-war, while streams
of copper-rich, blue blood, cool as the night sea,
course through my three hearts, my mollusk brains
will feel more keenly their relation to the world
than any brainless mussel ever felt

while fattening on a farmer's rope. We like
to think we choose, and then we choose to harm
ourselves and bring pain to the ones we say
we love. My next life may be brief. Male octopus
and female couple once and die. The male caressingly
plants sperm under the mantle of his mate,
who kills and eats him if she finds the woo subpar.
If he does well, however, he will himself
release from optic glands like our pituitaries
hormones which at other times spur puberty
or hunger, and now bring about swift aging
to the point of death. The female, meanwhile,
with the male's third right arm broken off inside her,
seeks the lair where she can tend her eggs
while fasting for some weeks until they hatch
and she too dies. With luck my soul, inside
the just-hatched larval mollusk of my choice,
will drift for days among great clouds of plankton,
much as the octopus from my last sushi now drifts,
vagrant somewhere in the salt depth of this thought.

Fig Preserves

Two women while they talk peel figs.
To keep them whole, with stems and underskins
intact, they soak in limewater, and slow-cook

in spiced syrup until clear. Jars of these
with curls of cinnamon and lemon wheels
in amber, anyone can see, are works of art—

each fig a work of art. One woman tells
wild stories from her past, which the other cannot
understand as art or even as a gift, but takes

to be raw life. I liked my figs raw as a boy.
I liked tearing them apart just picked.
The storyteller in the scene above is poor

and black, or colored, as she puts it,
and the listener is rich and white. The rich one
staggers into grief and guilt. A tumor grows

inside the poor one's brain. And neither asks
for help. And both provide. My mother,
having lived this, wrote the scene in her last novel

so that to understand it, as the prophet said,
is to believe. My mother gropes
at eighty-nine for words to tell me

how her father hung their tree with pots
and pans, and from the porch late afternoons
and Sundays, when he saw the birds

and squirrels come back for figs, how
he would set things clanging with a yank
on the bell cord tied to a limb. He kept watch

every year, to save figs for dessert and canning.
When my mother tries to talk, some days,
the words are ripe and easy on the stem,

the way they were when she wrote stories,
back when I would help pick figs,
and she would let me eat more than I picked.

NOTES

5 "The Other World"—The site of one of the earliest known chariot burials is in Russia near Kazakhstan, not far from Krivoye Ozero, or Crooked Lake.

9 "After the Snow Squall"—When earthlight suffuses the darkened area inside the crescent of a new moon, the new moon has the old moon in her arm.

15 "We Could Say Οὐρανός"—Uranus (OOR-ah-noos in Latin) is visible to the naked eye, but is so faint and moves so slowly that it was not known to be a planet until the eighteenth century.

25 "Observations from a Hillside Stairway on the Day of Atonement, Just Before My Wife and Daughters Break Their Fast"—Rags, in poker lingo, are cards of no particular value. James Erwin was a nineteenth-century circuit rider from northern New York State. His father, a Presbyterian minister, disapproved when James as a boy began to preach the more liberal tenets of Methodism.

40 "The Nationality of Neptune"—William Herschel discovered that the faintest planet visible to the naked eye was a planet. He named it after the English king. A Swede called it Neptune. A German called it Uranus, and said that its orbit was affected by another planet, sighted later on the strength of calculations made by a Frenchman. The Frenchman wanted to name the more distant planet after himself, but he had been calling it Neptune before the sighting. This time Neptune stuck.

41 "The Arctic Vortex on Snooks Pond, 2014"—A winter that is cooler than usual in parts of the United States may be warmer than usual in the Northern Hemisphere as a whole. For the planet, 2014 was the warmest year since 1850 when detailed record keeping began. The next five years were the warmest ever recorded and July 2019 was the warmest month. Almost everyone who has stud-

ied climate science attributes the rise in planetary temperature to carbon emission from human activities.

42 "Apologies to the Dead"—The word *apology* here means advocacy to an unreceptive audience, as in the *Apology of Socrates*. Children with precocious ovulation have given birth as early as the age of five. According to family records, Mary Howard at the age of eight gave birth to her first son, whose father was then twenty-five.

52 "Near Saturn"—The largest of Saturn's moons, Titan, is the one moon in our solar system with an atmosphere. At the temperatures and pressures under Titan's crust, water mixed with ammonia may be liquid, but at the surface water is ice. Lakes of ethane and methane there are the only bodies of surface liquid known to exist apart from those on Earth. A benzene snowflake may fall into an ethane lake and sink intact. In the rings of Saturn moonlets are detectable as propeller-shaped windows of darkness. Astrophysicists call the sources of discrepancies in our best equations *dark matter* and *dark energy*. According to their best hypothesis, these mysterious presences make up about 95 percent of the universe.

53 "*Lingerie Femme* and the Vagaries of Pronunciation"—My father liked reference books and provocative assertions. The diatribe in this poem appeals to me most when I hear it in his voice.

60 "A Voter from Mississippi Considers the State Constitution"— The opening phrase of this poem alludes to the love described as the greatest virtue in 1 Corinthians 13. Most state constitutions make mental competence prerequisite for voting. Some states deny "idiots and insane persons" the right to vote. Legal definitions for these terms, also used in immigration law, have been disputed.

62 "A Cat Lover's Guide to *The Bell Curve*"—Apart from conditions where people raise them for slaughter, pigs are protective of their young and clean in their habits, with an intelligence about equal to that of dogs. Cats regard pigs and dogs as inferior.

70 "From Anyte of Tegea"—This translation is dedicated to my friends Samuel Gruber and his late wife, Judith Meighan. Details

about the spear have been added, since it is no longer reasonable to assume a reader's familiarity with such things. Proper names from the Greek have been omitted.

72 "Bananas"—In some photographs the golden langur looks like Henrik Ibsen. This impression, and other details in some of these poems, may not be strictly factual.

74 "The Moons of Jupiter"—Patsy Cline died on March 5, 1963. Richard Kenneth Haxton Sr. died on March 5, 1970. When *Voyager I* made its closest approach to Jupiter on March 5, 1979, it photographed two previously undetected Jovian moons.

75 "Don't Get Me Wrong"—To label villages targeted for bombing as "concentrations of the enemy aggressor" and then to refer to hundreds of thousands of civilians killed as "collateral damage" is *microaggression* in one of the more recent senses of the term. Starbuck's poem "Of Late" addresses that misrepresentation.

79 "The Bewilderment"—According to current scholarship on the Johns associated with scripture, the baptist, the disciple, the evangelist, the epistolist, and the revelator seem to be five different people. In one version of the story of Eden, Lilith, the first woman, created equal to Adam, leaves the Garden when he insists that she lie under him during intercourse, not on top. Commander Peppitt's note on the use of the word *nookie* among men in the Royal Navy is in Partridge's *Dictionary of Slang*. John the Baptist appears in a leather girdle eating locusts and wild honey in Matthew 3:4. The description of locusts with stingers and human faces comes from Revelation 9:7.

83 "Transit of Venus, 1882"—The writings of Emily Dickinson might have remained unknown if not for the dedication of her brother Austin's lover, Mabel Loomis Todd, who worked for years after the poet's death editing the poems and securing their first publication. Her work helped the poems find an audience in the seven decades before the original language was restored. Mabel Loomis Todd was also an accomplished musician, artist, writer, and conservation activist.

91 "Where But to Think Is to Be Full of Sorrow"—In this poem a man about to be reincarnated prefers the more active intelligence of an octopus to the mentality of other mollusks, such as mussels and clams. The author, on the other hand, feels drawn toward flickerings of consciousness at the subatomic and super galactic levels.

ACKNOWLEDGMENTS

Thanks to the editors of the following magazines for publishing poems from this collection: *Agni* ("Catullus, Carmen III," "Catullus, Carmen VIII," "From Anyte of Tegea"); *The Atlantic* ("The Other World"); *Corresponding Voices* ("Love and Empire," "Message, 1944" [under the title "Information, 1944"], "The Cormorant at Snooks Pond," "Qoheleth," "Unlit Kitchen, 5 A.M."); *The Georgia Review* ("Olm," "Where But to Think Is to Be Full of Sorrow"); *Michigan Quarterly Review* ("Oceanic," "To the Water Bear"); *New England Review at Breadloaf* website ("Mister Toebones," "Tracks Everywhere at Noon"); *The Paris Review* ("A Cat Lover's Guide to *The Bell Curve*"); *Ploughshares* ("The Arctic Vortex at Snooks Pond, 2014"); *The Progressive* ("Don't Get Me Wrong"); *Smartish Pace* ("The Featherbed"); *Southern Humanities Review* ("A Voter from Mississippi Considers the State Constitution"); *Virginia Quarterly Review* ("Observations from a Hillside Stairway on the Day of Atonement, Just Before My Wife and Daughters Break Their Fast," "Bananas," "The Journal of Dr. Beaurieux"); *Waxwing* ("To Abu Ali al-Hasan ibn al-Hasan ibn al-Haytham," "Copernicus"); and *The Yale Review* ("*Lingerie Femme* and the Vagaries of Pronunciation").

Thanks to Deborah Garrison, whose editing of four collections of my poems has been the most constant support of my life in publishing. Todd Portnowitz has been a crucial help in bringing out this book. My wife Francie and our three children have given me the only world where these poems could have come to be.

A Note About the Author

Brooks Haxton has published nine books of poetry, a nonfiction
account of his son's career in high-stakes poker, and translations
from Greek, French, and German. His poems have appeared in *The
Atlantic, The New Yorker, The Paris Review,* and elsewhere, and
his nonfiction has been featured in *The New York Times Sunday
Magazine.* He wrote the script for a film on the life and work of
Tennessee Williams, broadcast in the *American Masters* series.
A recipient of grants and awards from the National Endowment
for the Arts, the National Endowment for the Humanities, the
Guggenheim Foundation, and others, Haxton has taught for
many years in the graduate creative writing programs of Syracuse
University and Warren Wilson College.

A Note About the Type

The text of this book was set in Sabon, a typeface designed by Jan Tschichold (1902–1974), the well-known German typographer. Designed in 1966 and based on the original designs by Claude Garamond (ca. 1480–1561), Sabon was named for the punch cutter Jacques Sabon, who brought Garamond's matrices to Frankfurt.

Composed by North Market Street Graphics, Lancaster, Pennsylvania
Printed and bound by Friesens Printing, Altona, Canada
Designed by Maria Carella